ROMANTASY COLOURING BOOK

HODDER CHILDREN'S BOOKS
First published in Great Britain in 2025 by
Hodder and Stoughton Limited

© 2025 Hodder & Stoughton

Illustrations by Dynamo Limited
Additional images © Shutterstock

All rights reserved. A CIP catalogue record for this book is available from the British Library.

ISBN: 978-1-444-98514-6

10 9 8 7 6 5 4 3 2 1

Printed in China

Hodder Children's Books
An imprint of
Hachette Children's Group
Part of Hodder and Stoughton Limited
Carmelite House, 50 Victoria Embankment
London EC4Y 0DZ

An Hachette UK Company
www.hachette.co.uk
www.hachettechildrens.co.uk

The authorised representative in the EEA is Hachette Ireland, 8 Castlecourt Centre, Dublin 15, D15 XTP3, Ireland (email: info@hbgi.ie)

Romantasy Colouring Book

HOW TO USE THIS BOOK

The paper in this book is suitable for colouring with pencils or markers.

If you are using markers, it's a good idea to place a sheet of thick paper or card behind the page you're colouring to stop the colour bleeding through onto other pages.

TIPS FOR COLOURING IN

Plan ahead - Choose your materials and test them first, especially if you're using markers. Make a colour chart to see how the colours blend and look next to each other.

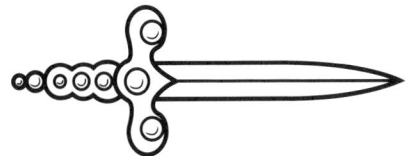

Gently does it - Try to use gentle strokes in a single direction. Build up the colour gradually, working from the outside in.

Layer up - Apply multiple layers of colour to achieve darker shades and richer tones. Great for creating highlights and shadows.

TIPS FOR COLOURING IN

Stay sharp - Don't forget to sharpen those pencils for more control and accuracy in your lines. Try using the side of the lead for larger areas and the point for small details.

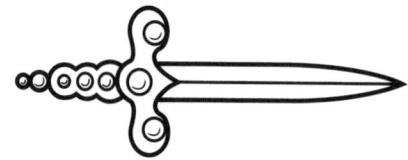

Mix it up - Why not experiment and combine different materials. Pencil and pen? Crayons and paint? Go for it!

Have fun! Relax, enjoy the process and let that creative energy flow!

TEST YOUR PENS

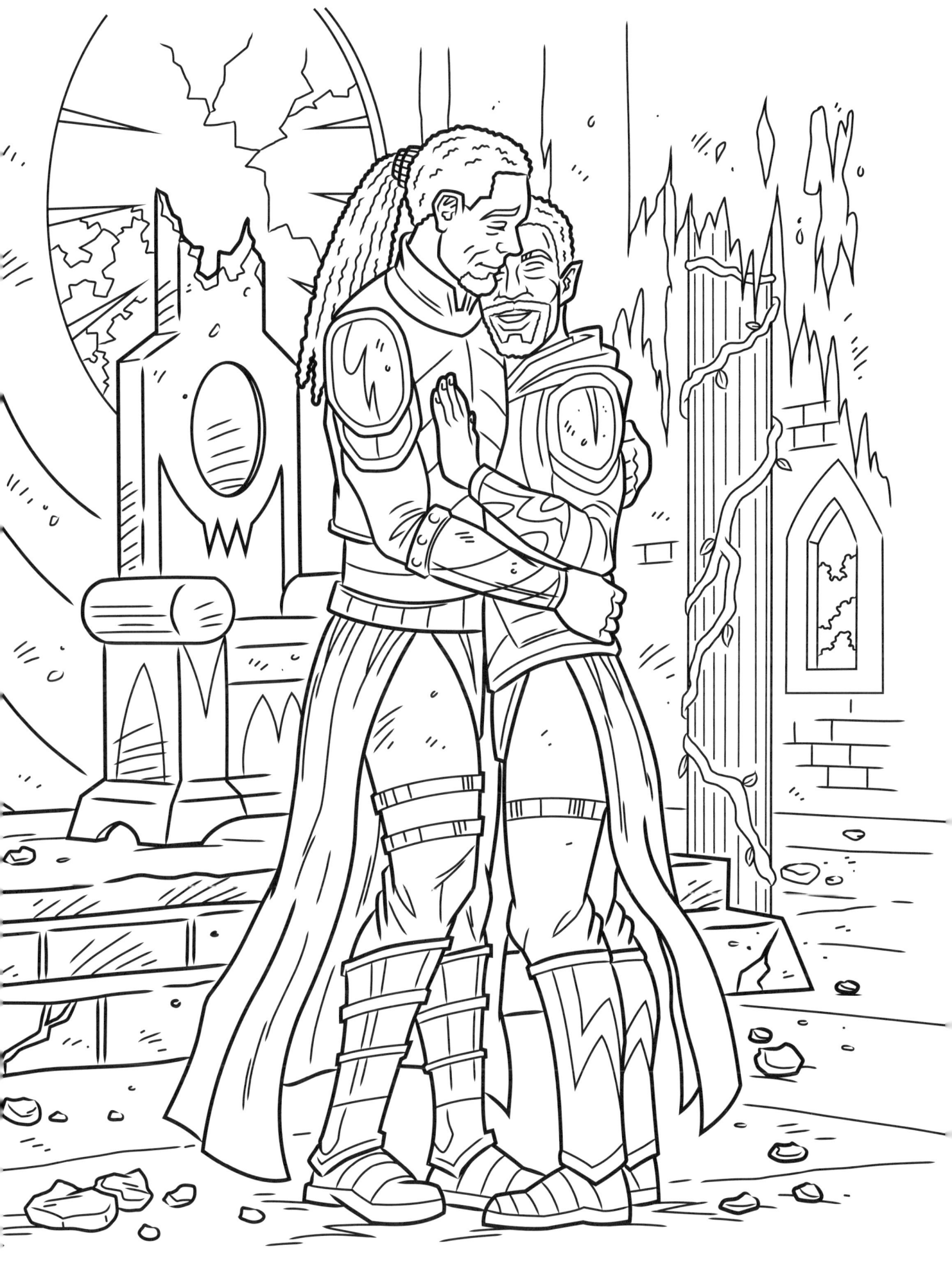